ISBN 1-84135-276-4

First published 2004
Second impression 2006

Published by Award Publications Limited,
The Old Riding School, The Welbeck Estate,
Worksop, Nottinghamshire. S80 3LS

Printed in Malaysia

MY FIRST PICTURE DICTIONARY

Illustrated by Terry Burton

AWARD PUBLICATIONS LIMITED

a is for animals

Animals that live with us or work for us are called **domestic** animals.

Hamster

Some are kept as **pets**:

Dog

Some are kept on **farms**:

Ram and Sheep

Pig

Many animals do not live with us; these are **wild** animals. You can see some of them in the countryside and others at the **zoo**. If you are very lucky, you could go on a **safari** in Africa. This is a special holiday to see the animals.

Wild animals in the **countryside**:

Deer

Hare

Wild animals from **other lands**:

Beaver from Canada

Koala from Australia

Lion from Africa

There are over 80 animal words in the dictionary. How many can you find?

Aa

Abacus

The abacus is a counting-frame that has been used for doing sums for many hundreds of years.

Abbey

A community of monks used to live and worship in an abbey.

Accident

James had an accident and fell off his bike.

Acorn

An acorn is the fruit of an oak tree.

Acrobat

These acrobats perform exciting balancing acts in a show.

Aeroplane

People can fly to foreign countries in an aeroplane.

Alligator

An alligator is a reptile that has a long mouth with many sharp teeth, and a long tail.

abcdefghijklmnopqrstuvwxyz

Alphabet

Our **alphabet** has 26 letters and we use them to make up all our words.

abcdefg
hijklmn
opqrstu
vwxyz

Ambulance

An **ambulance** takes ill or injured people to hospital.

Anchor

The **anchor** is very heavy and when it digs into the sea bed it will stop the boat floating away.

Angel

I was an **angel** in my school nativity play.

Animal

An **animal** is a living thing that can move about.

Ant
Anteater

Ants are insects that live in large groups in nests or ant-hills.
An **anteater** uses its long, sticky tongue to pick up ants to eat.

Antelope

Antelopes live in hot countries and look like deer.

Antlers

Deer grow hard horns called **antlers** on their heads.

abcdefghijklmnopqrstuvwxyz

Apple

An apple is a crunchy, juicy fruit which grows on a tree.

Apron

We wear aprons to protect our clothes.

Aquarium

An aquarium is a glass tank for keeping fish in, and a place where we can go and see them.

Archer

An archer is a person who shoots with a bow and arrow.

Ark

There are two of each kind of animal to play with in a Noah's ark.

Armchair

An armchair is a comfortable chair to sit in.

Armour

Knights of old wore armour for protection when fighting.

9

abcdefghijklmnopqrstuvwxyz

Artist

The **artist** is painting a picture of a church.

Assistant

The **assistant** helped me get a box of cornflakes from the top shelf.

Astronaut

An **astronaut** travels into space in a space rocket.

Athlete

An **athlete** is good at running or swimming or any other kind of sport.

Avalanche

An **avalanche** is a mass of snow, ice and rock which slides down a mountain.

Axe

The woodcutter is using a sharp **axe** to cut down the trees.

b is for birds

Bb

There are many different kinds of birds, and you can see them everywhere - in **towns**, in the **countryside**, at a **zoo**, on **holiday**, in the **garden**, on a **farm**. They live all over the world. They can be smaller than your hand, like a **hummingbird**, or taller than a man, like the **ostrich**.

Garden birds:

Blackbirds

Robin

Country or **seaside** birds:

Gull

Jackdaws

Farm birds:

Geese

Foreign birds:

Parrot from South America

Chickens

Penguins from Antarctica

There are over 30 bird words in the dictionary. How many can you find?

Bb

Baby

The boys must play quietly or they will wake the **baby** who is sleeping in the push-chair.

Badger

A **badger** lives underground in a set, or burrow, and comes out at night to hunt for food.

Baker

A **baker** makes bread for us to eat.

Bale

Hay is cut, collected and then stored in very large square or round **bales**.

Ball

A **ball** is used in many different games – football, rugby, cricket, tennis, hockey and lots of others.

Ballet

A **ballet** is a dance that can tell a story, usually with the help of music.

Balloon

Balloons like these use hot air to carry them into the sky.

abcdefghijklmnopqrstuvwxyz

Banana

A **banana** is a long fruit which has a yellow skin and a soft inside.

Bandage

I am a nurse today, and I'm putting **bandages** on my dog.

Banjo

A **banjo** is a musical instrument which looks like a round guitar.

Barbecue

We cook sausages and beefburgers on the **barbecue** in our garden.

Barge

A **barge** like this used to carry loads from town to town along rivers and round the coast.

Bark

The outer layer of a tree is called **bark**.

Barn

On a farm, tractors or hay can be kept in the **barn**.

Barrel

These **barrels** are loaded with water and food, ready to go on to the sailing ship.

abcdefghijklmnopqrstuvwxyz

Basket

We are picking apples and putting them in our **basket**.

Bat

The **bat** is a small creature that flies about at night.

A **bat** is used to hit a ball in many games.

Bead

Different coloured **beads** can be threaded on to a cord to make a necklace or bracelet.

Beak

The hard part of a bird's mouth is called a **beak**.

Beam

The **beam** of light from the car's headlamps shows up the dark road.

Bean

A **bean** is a long green pod, or the seed inside it, which we eat as a vegetable.

Bear

A **bear** is a large wild animal, with brown, black or white fur.

14

abcdefghijklmnopqrstuvwxyz

Beard

The shepherd has a thick **beard** on his face.

Beaver

The **beaver** has a flat tail, and builds its home in a stream or river from trees that it cuts down with its sharp teeth.

Bed

My brother and I sleep in bunk **beds**.

Bee
Beehive

Bees are insects that make honey, and they live in a **beehive**.

Beetle

A **beetle** is an insect which has hard, shiny wing-covers to protect its wings.

Bell

The sailor rings the **bell** to let everyone know what time it is.

Bench

We sit on the **bench** in the park to feed the birds.

Bicycle

We can ride our **bicycles** on the path through the park.

abcdefghijklmnopqrstuvwxyz

Binoculars

The birds seem bigger when I watch them through my **binoculars**.

Bird

A **bird** is a creature with wings, feathers and a beak, and most birds can fly.

Birthday

Everyone sang Happy **Birthday** to me before I blew out the candles on the cake.

Blackbird

The **blackbird** is a garden bird with a beautiful song; the male is black but the female has brown feathers.

Blackboard

I have written the sum on the **blackboard** with chalk.

Blacksmith

A **blacksmith** makes shoes for horses using hot metal.

Blanket

Mummy puts a **blanket** on my bed to keep me warm.

Blizzard

A **blizzard** is a very heavy snowstorm.

abcdefghijklmnopqrstuvwxyz

Blouse

We both have the same **blouse** on today.

Blue tit

Dad has put up a bird box in the garden for the **blue tits** to nest in.

Boat

A **boat** floats on the river or sea and has an engine or sails to make it move.

Bone

The dog is digging a hole to bury his **bone**.

Book

Daddy lent me this **book** about birds to read.

Boot

The kittens are playing with my wellington **boots**.

Bottle

Bottles can be made from plastic or glass, and some are used for medicines.

Bouquet

We bought Mummy a **bouquet** of flowers for her birthday.

Bow

The musician plays her violin with a **bow** and she is also wearing a **bow** in her hair.

Bowl

The ingredients for a cake are stirred together in the **bowl** before the mixture is put into a tin and cooked.

Box

My little brother likes to put his head in this **box**!

Bracelet

Mummy says I can wear her **bracelets** today.

Bread

We buy loaves of **bread** for making toast and sandwiches.

Bricks

The builders are using **bricks** to build this wall.

Bride
Bridegroom
Bridesmaid

The **bride** and **bridegroom** stand with the **bridesmaid** for the photographs to be taken.

Bridge

A **bridge** is built over a river, a railway or a road so we are able to cross it.

Broom

I am sweeping the path with Daddy's big **broom**.

Brush

My sister is using a **brush** to get rid of the tangles in my hair.

Bubbles

I can blow big, soapy **bubbles**.

Bucket

The **bucket** I was filling with water overflowed on the path.

Bulb

A **bulb** is planted for flowers in the spring, and a **bulb** in a lamp gives light.

abcdefghijklmnopqrstuvwxyz

Bull

A **bull** is the father of a calf; bulls, cows and calves are all cattle.

Bulldozer

This **bulldozer** has a snowplough on the front to clear away the snow after a blizzard.

Bun

The dog can smell the iced **buns** on the table and he would like one of them to eat.

Buoy

A **buoy** is used to mark channels of deep water for ships to follow.

Burrow

Rabbits make their home in a **burrow**.

Bus

This **bus** takes passengers round the city.

Bush

The **bush** in the garden is covered with flowers.

Butter

Butter is made from cream, and is delicious on toast with some honey.

Buttercup

Buttercups are golden yellow flowers that grow wild in fields or in the garden.

Butterfly

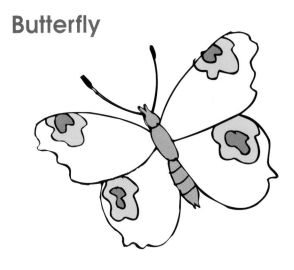

A **butterfly** is a delicate insect with beautiful wings.

Button

Buttons come in many different shapes and sizes, and help you keep your clothes on!

Cc

Cabbage

Cabbage is a green, leafy vegetable that we can cut up and cook.

Cactus

The cactus is a plant that grows in hot, dry countries because it does not need a lot of water.

Cage

I keep my guinea-pig in a cage.

Cake

Mum made a cake and I can't wait to taste it!

Calculator

I can add up, subtract and do all sorts of sums on my calculator.

Calendar

My mum writes down all the birthdays and anniversaries on our calendar.

Calf

A calf is a young cow.

abcdefghijklmnopqrstuvwxyz

Camel

The **camel** can go great distances in the desert without drinking water.

Camp

We put up our tents and made **camp** in a quiet field.

Canal

Boats and barges use **canals** to travel from town to town.

Candle

He lit the **candle** with a match so that they could see in the dark.

Canoe

A **canoe** is a light, narrow boat with no engine, paddled by one or more people.

Car

Mum takes me to school in the **car** when it is raining.

Caravan

This old **caravan** would be pulled by a horse, not a car.

Cargo

Cargo is carried in container ships from country to country.

abcdefghijklmnopqrstuvwxyz

Carpenter

The carpenter cuts, saws and smooths wood in his workshop.

Carpet

The carpet on my bedroom floor is green, like grass!

Carriage

Before cars were invented, people used to travel in a horse and carriage.

Carrot

A carrot is a long orange vegetable, which can be eaten raw or cooked.

Cart

This cart was used to take things to market.

Castle

This castle has a moat round it which used to keep enemies out in olden days.

Cat

The cat is watching the bird which it tried to catch.

Caterpillar

One day, these caterpillars will change into butterflies or moths.

Cave

Thousands of years ago, before man could build houses, people used to live in caves.

Chain

The padlock and chain is used to keep the gate shut and locked.

Chair

When it is cold outside, my grandpa likes to sit by the fire on this old wooden chair.

Cheese

Cheese can be made from cows', sheep's or goats' milk, and comes in different shapes, flavours and colours.

Cheetah

The cheetah is the fastest animal on land.

Chef

The chef is cooking in his kitchen.

Chicken

Chickens live in the farmyard, and lay eggs for us to eat.

Chimney

This house has very tall chimneys.

25

Chimpanzee

A **chimpanzee** is an ape in the same family as the gorilla and the orang-utang.

Choir

The boys in the **choir** sing out loudly.

Church

People go to the **church** in the village to worship God.

Class

This **class** of children is learning about different parts of the world.

Cliff

The seagulls make their nests on the **cliffs** overlooking the sea.

Clock

My alarm **clock** is set to wake me up early!

Cloud

Big grey **clouds** in the sky sometimes give us rain.

abcdefghijklmnopqrstuvwxyz

Clown

A clown paints his face with a big smile and makes us laugh.

Coal

Coal is dug out of the ground and burned on a fire to keep a room warm.

Coat

These coats are too big for us!

Cobweb

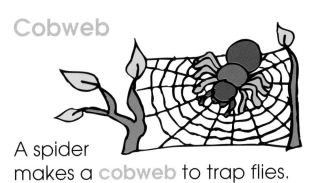

A spider makes a cobweb to trap flies.

Cockerel

A cockerel is a male chicken.

Comb

Thomas watched his sister as she tidied his hair with a comb.

Compass

Using a compass to give us the direction, and a map, we can travel from place to place.

Cone

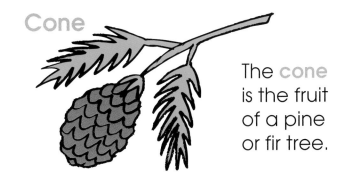

The cone is the fruit of a pine or fir tree.

27

abcdefghijklmnopqrstuvwxyz

Cow

A cow eats grass, and produces milk for us to drink and to make butter, cheese and yoghurt.

Cowboy

Cowboys look after cattle in the Wild West of America.

Crab

The crab is a creature with two large claws that lives in the sea.

Cracker

We are pulling crackers under the tree at Christmas time.

Crane

A crane is used for moving heavy loads.

Crayon

Crayons are made of wax and I can use them for drawing as they make less mess than paint.

Cricket

A cricket is an insect that makes a chirping noise by rubbing its hard forewings together.

abcdefghijklmnopqrstuvwxyz

Cricket

To win a cricket match, one team has to score more runs than the other.

Crocodile

A crocodile is a reptile similar to an alligator, having a long tail and a large mouth with lots of teeth in it.

Crow

The carrion crow looks for dead animals or steals other birds' eggs and chicks for its food.

Crown

I am queen today, so it is my turn to wear the crown.

Cupboard

I am looking for something in the cupboard.

Curtain

Mum pulls the curtains when I go to bed.

Cutlery

Cutlery is the knives, forks and spoons we use for eating our food.

Cymbals

Clash! go the cymbals, while the drum goes *rat-a-tat-tat!*

Dd

Daffodil
Daisy

The **daffodil** has a yellow trumpet-like flower on a tall green stalk, and **daisies** are small white flowers that grow in the grass.

Dam

A **dam** is built across a river to hold back the water or to prevent flooding.

Dance

These men are doing a Morris **dance**, a traditional dance.

Dart

John's third **dart** hit the bull's-eye and won the game.

Decoration

My brother and I are putting up the Christmas **decorations** this year.

Deer

Deer are shy animals that often live in woodlands.

Dentist

The **dentist** looks after our teeth.

30

Desert

A desert is a very dry place, where few plants and animals can live.

Desk

I keep my books and schoolwork in my desk.

Detective

In stories about the detective Sherlock Holmes, he always manages to solve the crimes.

Dial

The face of a clock is also known as the dial.

Diamond

A diamond is a precious stone often used in jewellery.

Dice

A dice has six sides numbered from one to six by spots on its six sides, and is used in all sorts of board games.

Dictionary

This book is a dictionary, which is used to find words, their meanings and their spellings.

Dinghy

A dinghy is a small boat propelled by a small motor, by oars or by sails.

31

abcdefghijklmnopqrstuvwxyz

Dinosaur

Dinosaurs were reptiles that lived millions of years ago and ate meat or plants.

Diver

A diver wears a rubber suit and breathing equipment so that he can swim underwater.

Doctor

A doctor looks after us when we are ill, and prescribes medicine for us if we need it.

Dog

A dog is an animal that often lives with us as a pet.

Dolphin

A dolphin is a graceful sea creature with a beaklike snout, which breathes air.

Donkey

A donkey is an animal that looks like a horse, but it is smaller and has much longer ears.

Door

There is a shiny little knocker on our front door.

Dough

Mum said I could knead the dough but it's sticking to my hands!

abcdefghijklmnopqrstuvwxyz

Dragon

Fire-breathing and flying dragons appear in many different stories, but they do not really exist.

Drawer

The kitten has found a new home for itself in my drawer.

Drum

The bandsman can beat the drums very loudly but it does not disturb the horses.

Duck

The duck is a bird that swims on ponds, lakes and rivers. We often feed ducks in the park.

Dungarees

My little sister likes to wear her blue dungarees in the garden.

Dungeon

Dungeons in castles were used to hold prisoners in olden days.

Duster

I use the duster and polish to make the table shine.

Ee

Eagle

An eagle is a bird with very good eyesight that uses its sharp beak and claws to catch its food.

Earth

We live on the planet Earth, the third planet in the solar system.

Easel

An artist uses an easel to hold his paper or canvas while he is painting.

Egg

An egg is the first stage of life for many living creatures, such as birds, snakes, reptiles, insects and fish.

Elephant

An elephant is a very large animal with big flapping ears and a long trunk, which lives in India or Africa.

Embroidery

Pretty designs sewn on to material with coloured threads are called embroidery.

abcdefghijklmnopqrstuvwxyz

Engine

This engine is a steam locomotive, and is used to pull carriages along a track.

Envelope

We receive letters and packages through the post in ordinary or padded envelopes.

Escalator

An escalator is a moving staircase which goes up or down.

Eskimo

An Eskimo or Inuit used to live in a house built of snow blocks, called an igloo.

Excavator

The excavator is digging a hole with its enormous shovel.

f is for food

Ff

Many people shop in a **supermarket** where you can buy all the sorts of food listed in this dictionary. But some people like to go to shops which sell only some sorts of food. These shops have special names.

Dairy:

Cheese

Milk

We can also buy our milk from a **milkman** who delivers it to our house on his **milk float**.

Butcher: Meat

Bakery:

Cakes

Bread

Greengrocer: Fruit

Apples

Vegetables

Potatoes

Cabbage

Fishmonger: Fish

How many other food words can you find in the dictionary?

Ff

Factory

All sorts of things can be made in a **factory**.

Fairy

Daddy puts the **fairy** at the top of our Christmas tree.

Farm
Farmer

The **farmer** grows crops and looks after animals on the **farm**.

Feather

Birds are covered with **feathers** which keep them warm and dry, and help the birds to fly.

Fence

A **fence** is built to hold animals in a field, or to keep people out.

Ferry

We put our car on the **ferry** when we go across the English Channel to France.

abcde**f**ghijklmnopqrstuvwxyz

Field

Either crops can be grown or animals kept in a **field**.

Fire

The camp **fire** burns brightly and keeps us warm.

Fireman

The **fireman** unreels the hose for water to put out the fire.

Firework

There was a **firework** display to celebrate the end of the fair.

Fish

Fish are creatures that swim in the sea. They cannot live on the land.

Fisherman

The **fisherman** uses his nets to catch fish for us to eat.

Flag

Every country has a different national **flag**. How many do you know?

Flamingo

A **flamingo** is a large bird with long legs for wading, and pink or red feathers.

Fleece

When sheep's wool is taken off in one piece the wool is called a **fleece**.

Flour

Flour is ground wheat, or other grains, and is used in cooking all sorts of things such as cakes, biscuits and bread.

Flower

The **flower** of a plant is where the seeds are made, and it is usually very pretty.

Foal

A **foal** is the young, or baby, of a horse.

Fog

It is very difficult to see in **fog** and cars must always put their lights on.

Food

We need to eat **food** every day to live.

Football

John is kicking the **football** to score a goal.

Forest

The **forest** is full of trees.

abcdefghijklmnopqrstuvwxyz

Fork

We use a **fork** to eat our food.

Fountain

Water gushes out of the top of a **fountain** and splashes down into a pool.

Fox

The **fox** is an animal like a dog, with a long bushy tail, which is usually seen in the evening and at night.

Frog

This **frog** has strong hind legs for jumping, and webbed feet to help it swim.

Fruit

Fruit is the part of plants and trees that contain the seeds, and is often good to eat.

Funnel

By using a **funnel** I can easily pour liquids into a bottle.

Furniture

Tables, chairs, cupboards, beds, wardrobes, armchairs and settees are all **furniture**.

Gg

Galleon

This **galleon** sailed the high seas in the days before ships had engines.

Gallery

We are visiting the art **gallery** to see the different pictures.

Galley

This Viking **galley** could sail across the sea, or be rowed by teams of men with oars.

Garage

We keep our car in the **garage** next to our house.

Garden

We grow plants and trees in our **garden** and there is a big lawn to play on.

Gate

The postman has to open the **gate** to walk up to our front door.

Giant

A **giant** in a fairy-tale is much bigger than normal people.

41

abcdefghijklmnopqrstuvwxyz

Giraffe

The **giraffe** has a long neck and legs so it can feed on the leaves at the top of the trees.

Glasses

Grandad has to wear **glasses** to read his book.

Glove

We wear **gloves** to keep our hands warm and dry when the weather is cold and wet.

Gnome

Some people have a garden **gnome** by their pond.

Goat

This young **goat** is called a kid. Goats' milk can be used to make cheese.

Go-kart

There is a track near us where we can race our **go-karts**.

Goldfish

I have a tank in my room and I keep **goldfish** in it.

Golf

Golf is a game played with long clubs and a small ball which is hit into holes.

abcdefghijklmnopqrstuvwxyz

Goose

A **goose** is a big farm bird, and it makes a good 'guard dog' because it will hiss and peck at strangers.

Gorilla

A **gorilla** is an ape, like a chimpanzee, and it lives in Africa.

Grape

Grapes can be eaten raw, dried as raisins and sultanas, or used to make wine.

Grapefruit

A **grapefruit** is a large yellow citrus fruit which is usually cut in half and eaten at breakfast.

Guard

This Swiss **Guard** protects the Pope in the Vatican City in Italy.

Guide

The **guide** leads the way over the mountains.

Guitar

My friend is teaching me to play the **guitar**.

Gull

A **gull** is a seabird which now comes inland to find food on rubbish-tips.

Hh

Half

The boy has painted his face **half** green and half white to support his football team.

Hammer

The craftsman uses a **hammer** to hit nails into wood, or to beat metal into shape.

Hammock

On a hot sunny day, it is lovely to relax in a **hammock** strung between two trees.

Hamper

We take a **hamper** of food on a picnic.

Hamster

The **hamster** is a small furry animal with cheek pouches for carrying food back to its nest.

Handkerchief

You can use your **handkerchief** for things other than blowing your nose!

Hangar

Aeroplanes are kept in the **hangar** on an airfield.

abcdefghijklmnopqrstuvwxyz

Hanger

Mum found a hanger for me to put my jacket on.

Harbour

The fishing boats come into harbour when they have finished their work.

Hare

A hare looks like a large rabbit with long ears and it can run very fast.

Harp

A harp is a musical instrument with many strings, which is played with both hands.

Harvester

A combine harvester is used by farmers to cut grain and pack the straw into bales.

Hat

We wear hats when it is raining to keep our hair dry and when it is sunny to protect our heads.

Hawk

A hawk is a bird of prey that catches other birds and small animals to feed on.

Hedge

When Dad cuts the hedge, I put the clippings in the wheelbarrow.

abcdefghijklmnopqrstuvwxyz

Hedgehog

A **hedgehog** is a small animal which has spines all over its back to protect it.

Helicopter

A **helicopter** flies in the air by using blades that spin round on top of it.

Helmet

A **helmet** is worn to protect the head.

Hill

The village is in the valley and the farmhouse is halfway up the **hill**.

Hippopotamus

A **hippopotamus** is a very large animal that lives in Africa and spends most of its life in water.

Holly

The **holly** tree has prickly leaves and bright red berries.

Honey

Honey is a sweet food, made by bees, which we can spread on bread.

Hook

I hang my cap on my **hook** when I go to school.

46

abcdefghijklmnopqrstuvwxyz

Hoop

Bowling a hoop is an old-fashioned game that our great-grandparents played.

Horse

This large horse is a shire horse, and they were once used to pull carts and ploughs.

Hose

The hose is connected to the tap so that Dad can easily water the garden.

Hospital

People are sent to hospital when they are ill or injured.

House

Your house is the building where you live with your family.

Hovercraft

A hovercraft travels over the ground or water on a cushion of air.

Hummingbird

A hummingbird beats its wings so fast that it seems to hang in the air when it is feeding on nectar.

Ice

Ice is frozen water, and we can put ice cubes in our drinks to keep them cold.

Ice cream

I love having ice cream in a cornet – it makes such a mess!

Iceberg

An iceberg is a lump of ice which floats around on the sea, and can be bigger than a ship.

Icicle

Icicles are made of running or dripping water that has frozen as it is dropping.

Igloo

Igloos are made by Inuits, or Eskimos, from large blocks of hard snow that are cut and stacked like bricks to make a warm little house.

Ink

When we write with a pen and ink we try not to make a mess.

abcdefgh**i**jklmnopqrstuvwxyz

Insect

An **insect** is a small creature with six legs, and some, like this bee, have wings.

Instrument

These drawing **instruments** are used for making accurate diagrams or plans.

A horn is a musical **instrument** that we play by blowing in a mouthpiece.

Invitation

You are invited to my party on Saturday. LUCY

Lucy sent me an **invitation** to her party on Saturday.

Island

An **island** is a piece of land entirely surrounded by water – Great Britain is an island.

Ivory

An elephant has tusks of **ivory** which is made of the same material as your teeth.

j is for jobs

Many people go to places with special names to do their jobs.

Assistant: **Shop**

Chef and **Waiter**: **Restaurant**

Doctor and **Nurse**: **Hospital**

Blacksmith: **Forge**

Dentist and **Doctor**: **Surgery**

Baker: **Bakery**

Cowboy: **Ranch**

Teacher: **School**

Clown: **Circus**

How many other jobs can you find in the dictionary?

Jj

Jackdaw

A jackdaw is a bird that likes to collect glittering objects and hide them in its nest.

Jacket

A jacket is a short coat that can either do up with a zip or with buttons.

Jam

My mum has made some strawberry jam and when it is cold I can have some on a slice of bread.

Jar

A jar is usually made of glass, and all sorts of foods can be kept inside them.

Jeans

Jeans are tough, hard-wearing trousers made of a material called denim.

Jeep

A jeep is a strong vehicle that can be driven over rough ground.

abcdefghijklmnopqrstuvwxyz

Jet

A jet is a plane that can travel through the air very quickly.

Jewellery

Earrings, necklaces, rings, brooches and bracelets are all kinds of jewellery.

Jigsaw puzzle

A jigsaw puzzle is a picture on wood or card which has been cut into funny-shaped pieces.

Jockey

A jockey rides a horse in a race with other jockeys and their horses.

Juggler

A juggler can throw several balls up in the air at the same time and still catch them!

Jungle

This jungle is like a forest, with many trees and plants, but it is also very hot and rainy.

Kk

Kangaroo

A **kangaroo** is an animal from Australia that has big back feet, a strong tail and a pouch to carry its baby in.

Kennel

Our dog has his own little house, a **kennel**, in the garden.

Kettle

We boil water in a **kettle** for hot water to make tea or coffee.

Key

The middle **key** on my keyring is for my front door.

King

A **king** is the ruler of a land, and the king of hearts is one of the four kings in a deck of cards.

Kingfisher

The **kingfisher** is a beautifully coloured bird that catches fish to eat.

Kiss

The baby is giving his mother a **kiss** to show that he loves her.

abcdefghijklmnopqrstuvwxyz

Kitchen

The **kitchen** is the room in the house where we do our cooking.

Kite

On a windy day we can fly a **kite** from the garden.

Kitten

A **kitten** is the young of a cat.

Knife

We use a **knife** to cut things, such as our food when we are eating.

Knight

A **knight** in the Middle Ages wore armour and rode a large horse into battle, fighting for his lord or his king.

Knitting

Granny does a lot of **knitting**, and this time she's making me a long scarf.

Knot

My big brother tied a **knot** in the rope to hold our swing in place.

Koala

A **koala** is an animal that looks like a small bear, which comes from Australia and feeds mainly on eucalyptus leaves.

Ll

Label

A **label** with my name on it will be tied to my suitcase when I go on holiday.

Lace

Lace is made from fine threads which are woven, twisted or knotted together to make a patterned fabric or edging.

Ladder

The window cleaner uses a **ladder** to reach the upstairs windows.

Ladle

The cook uses a **ladle** to pour custard into the bowls.

Ladybird

A **ladybird** is a small beetle which has red wing-covers with black spots.

Lake

A **lake** is a large stretch of water, much bigger than a pond.

Lamb

A **lamb** is the young of a sheep.

Lamp

A **lamp** is another word for a light, but it is usually an old-fashioned light.

Lather

My dad uses foam to make a **lather** on his chin before he shaves.

Lawn

The **lawn** is an area of cut grass beside a house.

Leaf

A **leaf** is the green part of a tree, plant or bush, but the leaves of a lot of trees change colour to red, yellow and brown in autumn.

Leak

Dad's hose has sprung a **leak**, so water is shooting out of the hole.

Leek

A **leek** is a vegetable in the onion family.

Lemon

A **lemon** is an oval pale yellow citrus fruit with a sour taste.

Leopard

A **leopard** is a large animal which belongs to the cat family and it has a spotted coat.

abcdefghijk**l**mnopqrstuvwxyz

Letter

I wonder if the postman has delivered a **letter** for me today, because I am waiting for one from my friend.

Library

A **library** is a place with many books that people can borrow to read at home.

Lifeboat

A **lifeboat** is used to rescue people at sea.

Lighthouse

This **lighthouse** is built on a dangerous part of the coast to warn ships away by flashing a bright light.

Lightning

We see **lightning** and hear thunder when a thunderstorm comes.

Lion

A **lion** is a large member of the cat family, which lives in a group called a pride.

abcdefghijklmnopqrstuvwxyz

Litter

We should throw our **litter** and rubbish into a bin.

Lizard

A **lizard** is a reptile with smooth, dry skin.

Lobster

A **lobster** is an edible sea creature with a hard shell and two large claws.

Lock

Turn the key in the **lock** and the door cannot be opened until it is unlocked.

Log

A **log** is a large piece of wood, sometimes the whole trunk of a tree.

Lollipop

I can't decide if I want an orange, yellow or red **lollipop**.

Loom

A **loom** is used to weave thread or yarn into a fabric, by hand or mechanically.

Luggage

We pack our suitcases with clothes and then take our **luggage** on holiday.

m is for music

Mm

There are many musical instruments in an orchestra and they can be played in different ways.

You use a bow to play a violin.

You push down the keys on a piano.

You blow a trumpet.

You use your fingers to play a guitar.

You rattle or tap a tambourine with your hand.

You hit a drum with drumsticks.

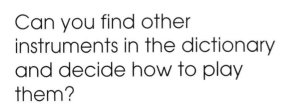

Can you find other instruments in the dictionary and decide how to play them?

You use your voice to sing in a choir.

Mm

Machine

With my sewing machine I can make all sorts of things, such as clothes or curtains.

Magician

We had a magician at my party and he could do magic tricks.

Magnet

I can pick up some metal objects with a magnet.

Magnifying glass

You can use a magnifying glass to make things look bigger.

Magpie

A magpie is a bird with black and white feathers; it is a member of the crow family.

Manger

Hay is put in the manger for animals to eat.

Map

If we follow the road marked on the map we will find our way to the church.

Mask

Tom and I each wore a mask for the school play.

Mast

The sails of a ship are held up by the mast.

Match

Grandad lit the candles on my birthday cake with a match.

Mattress

The mattress on this bed is very bouncy!

Maze

You have to follow the path round the maze to find the centre.

Meal

A meal is the food we eat at a certain time, such as breakfast, lunch, tea or dinner.

Meat

Meat is the part of an animal that can be eaten; most meat comes from cows, sheep, chickens and pigs.

Medal

I won a gold medal for my swimming.

abcdefghijkl**m**nopqrstuvwxyz

Medicine

I don't like taking my medicine, but it will make me better.

Menu

We look at the menu to see what food we can order when we go to a restaurant.

Mermaid

In Copenhagen, Denmark, there is a statue of Hans Andersen's Little Mermaid.

Microscope

A microscope is a scientific instrument used to look at very small things.

Milk

We drink milk, have it with our breakfast cereal, and in our tea and coffee.

Mirror

My naughty brother watched himself in the mirror as he put Mummy's lipstick on his face.

abcdefghijkl**m**nopqrstuvwxyz

Mitten

My **mittens** are like gloves without fingers, and they match my hat and coat.

Moat

We've built a sandcastle, and filled the **moat** with water.

Model

I'm now putting the mast on my **model** boat.

Mole

A **mole** is a small furry creature that lives underground, digging tunnels and making molehills.

Monkey

A **monkey** uses its tail and long arms and legs for swinging and climbing in the trees.

Monument

A **monument** is built to remind us of a person or an event; this one marks the place where the Fire of London began in 1666.

abcdefghijkl**m**nopqrstuvwxyz

Moon

The full **moon** is reflected in the water.

Moth

A **moth** is an insect that looks like a butterfly, but it flies around at night.

Motorbike

Some **motorbike** races, called scrambles, are run over rough ground through thick mud.

Mountain

A **mountain** is a very high rocky place.

Mouse

A **mouse** is a small animal called a rodent, which has a long tail and sharp teeth.

Mud

The water makes the **mud** by the river so sticky and gooey!

Muddle

My room is in a **muddle** again and my mum has told me to tidy it up.

Muscle

When I'm big, I'm going to have strong muscles in my arms, too.

Museum

We go to a museum to look at collections of historic, scientific or artistic things.

Music

I can now read music and play the notes on the piano.

Nn

Nail

A **nail** is hit through pieces of wood with a hammer, to hold them together.

Necklace

Emma is wearing a bead **necklace** round her neck.

Needle

We can sew material together with a **needle** and thread.

Neighbour

Neighbours often talk together over the fence.

Nest

Birds build a **nest** to lay their eggs and raise their young in.

Net

Will I catch a fish in my **net**?

Newspaper

People read a **newspaper** to find out what has been happening in the world.

abcdefghijklm**n**opqrstuvwxyz

Newt

We may find **newts** in our pond.

Nib

Different **nibs** in a pen will give different styles of writing.

Nightingale

A **nightingale** is a bird with a beautiful song that can be heard in the evening.

Notice-board

Posters and cards are pinned on a **notice-board** for everyone to read.

Nozzle

The fireman uses the **nozzle** on a hose to spray water at a fire.

Number

We use **numbers** for counting.

Nurse

The **nurse** puts a dressing on the cut to protect it.

Nut

The **nut** is the seed of some plants and trees, and can often be eaten.

Oo

Oak

An oak tree grows from a tiny acorn into a large tree.

Oar

Oars are used to make a boat move through the water.

Oasis

An oasis is a place in the desert where there is water and trees can grow.

Oast-house

Hops, used for making beer, are dried in oast-houses.

Obstacle

The children enjoy running through the obstacle course.

Octopus

The octopus has eight tentacles and lives in the sea.

Office

The secretary works at her word processor in an office.

abcdefghijklmn**o**pqrstuvwxyz

Officer

The officer on the horse is in charge of the soldiers.

Oil rig

An oil rig brings oil up from the sea bed and pipes it to land.

Old

These old things were made many years ago.

Onion

An onion is a vegetable that can be cooked or eaten raw.

Opossum

An opossum is a small animal that carries its young in a pouch.

Orange

An orange is a juicy citrus fruit which is delicious to eat!

Orchard

Fruit trees are grown in an orchard.

Orchestra

Many different musical instruments are played in an orchestra.

abcdefghijklmnopqrstuvwxyz

Organ

An organ is a large musical instrument. Air blown through many different sized pipes makes the sounds.

Oryx

An oryx is a kind of antelope that lives in Africa.

Ostrich

The ostrich is the largest bird in the world but it cannot fly.

Otter

The otter is a good swimmer and lives in holes in the riverbank.

Oven

Food is roasted or baked in an oven.

Owl

The owl is a bird that hunts at night and sleeps during the day.

Oxen

Oxen are used in some countries to plough and pull carts.

Oyster

The oyster is a shellfish which people can eat. Pearls can be found in some sorts of oysters.

Pp

Paddle

Each person has a **paddle** to guide the raft through the rapids.

Padlock

A **padlock** and chain are used to fasten this bicycle to the pole.

Page

Each **page** in this book has pictures as well as words on it.

Pail

A **pail** is another word for a bucket, and it can be used to hold water.

Paint

Paint is brushed on to the fence to protect it from the weather.

Pair

I have put on a **pair** of shoes, one on each foot.

Palace

A **palace** is the home of an important person, like a king or a queen.

Palm

Palm trees grow in warm and sunny places.

Panda

The **panda** is an animal from China that looks like a bear and feeds mainly on bamboo shoots.

Paper

My little brother has torn up the **paper**.

Parachute

A **parachute** is used when jumping from a plane as it lets the person float down to the ground.

Parcel

Mum has been given this **parcel** for her birthday – what can be inside the wrapping paper?

Park

We go to the **park** to play on the swings and slide.

abcdefghijklmnopqrstuvwxyz

Parrot

This brightly coloured **parrot** is called a macaw.

Passenger

The driver waits for the **passengers** to get on the bus.

Patch

I had a hole in my trousers and my mum put a **patch** over it.

Path

We follow the **path** to get down to the castle.

Pattern

These knitted jumpers have **patterns** on them.

Paw

The puppy is using its **paw** to pull the bag of sweets off the table.

Peacock

The **peacock** is a bird with magnificent fan-like tail feathers.

Pear

A **pear** is a fruit with a yellow or greenish skin.

abcdefghijklmnopqrstuvwxyz

Pelican

A **pelican** catches fish in its pouchy beak.

Pencil

We draw and write with **pencils**.

Penguin

Penguins are birds that cannot fly, and they live at the cold South Pole.

Perch

The canary is sitting on the **perch** in its cage.

Piano

The pianist is playing the **piano** in the band.

Picnic

Sitting on the grass and eating a **picnic** is a fine way to spend a sunny day.

Picture

This is a **picture** of my mummy and daddy standing outside my house!

abcdefghijklmnopqrstuvwxyz

Pier

The **pier** stretches out over the sea, and there is a theatre at the end of it.

Pig

A **pig** lives on a farm, it is an animal bred for its meat.

Pigeon

Pigeons are often seen in the centres of towns and cities.

Pillar

This ancient temple was built with many marble **pillars**.

Pilot

The **pilot** is the man or woman who flies an aeroplane.

Pineapple

A **pineapple** is a very juicy, tasty fruit.

Pirate

In olden days, **pirates** on a pirate ship used to attack and rob other ships at sea.

abcdefghijklmnopqrstuvwxyz

Pitchfork

The **pitchfork** was used to gather corn before the days of the combine harvester.

Planet

There are nine **planets**, including Earth, which revolve around the sun in our solar system.

Plank

A **plank** is a long, narrow piece of wood cut from a log.

Plant

Plants are grown for food, medicine, or for their flowers.

Platform

Passengers wait on the **platform** until the train comes in.

Plough

The horses pull this old **plough** across the field to break up the earth.

Plug

The **plug** on the lamp fits into a socket on the wall.

Plum

A **plum** is a sweet, juicy fruit with a hard stone, its seed, in the middle.

abcdefghijklmnopqrstuvwxyz

Pocket

Mum puts her keys and purse in the big **pockets** on her coat.

Polar Bear

The **polar bear** has white fur and lives in the ice and snow near the North Pole.

Police

The **police** protect and help the public; this policewoman has found a missing child.

Polish

If I **polish** my shoes, they will shine like new.

Pond

The ducks are swimming on the **pond**.

Pool

A swimming **pool** is a safe place to learn to swim.

Postbox

I am putting the postcards that Mum has written in the **postbox**.

abcdefghijklmnopqrstuvwxyz

Potato

A **potato** is a vegetable we can cook in various ways, making chips, or boiled, mashed or roast potatoes.

Pottery

Pottery can be made by a potter shaping clay on a fast-spinning wheel.

Pouch

A **pouch** is a useful place to keep small things, like coins or pens.

Present

Tom was very pleased with his **present** when he saw it was a radio-controlled racing car.

Prison

People who have done bad things are sent to **prison** as a punishment.

Prize

The **prize** for our team winning the match was a silver cup.

Propeller

An aeroplane can have one, two, or even four **propellers** to make it fly.

Puddle

When it rains, the water makes **puddles** on the ground for me to jump in!

abcdefghijklmnopqrstuvwxyz

Pump

Jack uses a **pump** to blow air into his bicycle's flat tyre.

Puncture

Daddy's car tyre has a **puncture** and it needs to be repaired before he can drive it any further.

Puppet

Ten little finger **puppets** to help me tell a story!

Puppy

A **puppy** is the young of a dog, and this naughty puppy has torn up a book.

Pyramid

These **pyramids** were built by the ancient Egyptians as tombs for their kings, called pharoahs.

Pyjamas

I wear my **pyjamas** in bed at night.

Qq

Quarter

This tomato has been cut into four **quarters**.

Quay

Several boats are moored up at the **quay**.

Queen

There are four **queens** in a pack of cards.

Queue

People form a **queue** to wait to buy their tickets.

Quill

Many years ago people used to write with a **quill** pen made from a quill, which is a large feather.

Quilt

This is a patchwork **quilt** for a bed.

Quiver

Arrows are kept safe and secure in a **quiver**.

Rr

Rabbit

A rabbit can be a wild animal or a pet, and it has soft fur and long ears.

Radio

When we listen to the radio we may hear music, stories or the news.

Raft

A raft can be made of logs tied together with rope, or from anything that floats.

Railway

Trains pulling carriages and trucks travel along the railway.

Rain

If we get caught in the rain we can get very wet.

Rainbow

Red, orange, yellow, green, blue, indigo and violet are the seven colours to be seen in a rainbow.

Rake

Dad uses a rake to gather up the dead leaves on the ground.

Ram

A ram is a male sheep, and it often has horns. Female sheep are called ewes.

Referee

The referee makes sure the football game is played fairly, and he has a loud whistle to blow if he sees a player doing something wrong.

Reflection

The kitten is looking at a reflection of herself in the mirror.

Refrigerator

We keep food cold in a refrigerator to help keep it fresh.

Reindeer

A reindeer is an animal from cold northern lands that can be used to pull sleighs and sledges through thick snow.

Restaurant

At a restaurant we can pay for a meal to be cooked for us.

Reward

LOST BEAR

£5 REWARD

A reward is a sum of money offered or given for information or the return of something stolen or lost.

abcdefghijklmnopqrstuvwxyz

Rhinoceros

A rhinoceros is a wild animal with one or two horns on its nose; it is becoming very rare because it is hunted for these horns.

Ribbon

We can use ribbons of different colours to tie in our hair, or to put round presents to make them look pretty.

Rider

The winning riders at the gymkhana are presented with trophies.

Ring

Rings which we wear on our fingers are made from gold or silver, and sometimes have precious stones in them.

River

The river flows alongside the field, and under the bridge, and I like to fish in it with a net.

Road

The road goes through the middle of town, past the houses and shops.

Robber

The robber is being chased by a policeman.

abcdefghijklmnopqrstuvwxyz

Robin

A robin is a small garden bird which has red breast feathers, giving it its popular name, 'robin redbreast'.

Rock

A rock is a large piece of stone.

Rocket

A rocket is used to launch a space shuttle to take astronauts to work in space or on a space station.

Roof

The roof is the covering on top of a house, and can be tiles, slate, or thatch.

Room

The rooms inside a house can be used for sleeping, cooking, sitting or working in.

Root

The root of a plant or tree is the part that grows underground, feeding the plant with goodness from the soil.

Rose

The rose is a plant grown in many gardens and there are hundreds of different varieties.

Ruin

A ruin is all that remains of some very old buildings and castles.

s is for sport

Ss

Many people play sports to keep fit and for fun. People who play to beat another person or team are a called competitors. Today many people play sports professionally which means it is their job. Places where people play sport have special names.

A jockey rides his horse on a racecourse.

A tennis player plays on a tennis court.

A golfer plays on a golf course.

A skier skis on a slope.

A cricketer plays on a pitch at a cricket ground.

A footballer plays at a stadium or a football pitch.

Athletics is a special collection of sports where people run races, jump, and try to throw things a long way. They go to a track at a stadium to compete.

A showjumper rides in a ring.

People who practise sport until they are very fit are called athletes.

Ss

Saddle

A **saddle** is a leather seat for a rider, with stirrups for the feet, and is put on a horse's back and fastened under its belly with a girth.

Safe

The thief cannot break the **safe** open to get at the money.

Sail

A ship may have **sails** made of nylon or canvas, which catch the wind and move the ship through the water.

Sandal

A **sandal** is an open shoe that we wear in the summer.

Sandwich

A **sandwich** is made from two slices of bread with a filling in between.

Satchel

The boy has put his books and homework in his **satchel** and is going to school.

Satellite

Man-made **satellites** orbiting the Earth can be used for communications, broadcasting, or to send us information on the weather.

Saucer

A saucer is a special dish that goes under a cup.

Sausage

Sausages and baked beans are easy to cook when we're camping.

Saw

Dad uses a saw to cut the wood for the shelves he is making.

Scales

Different types of scales are used to weigh different things, from light things such as letters and vegetables to much heavier things like people.

Scarecrow

A scarecrow stands in a field to scare away the birds.

School

We go to school to learn reading, writing, maths and lots of other subjects.

Scissors

We use scissors to cut things like paper, string or cloth.

Screw

A screw is used to hold things in place and is driven into wood by turning it with a screwdriver.

Seal

A seal is a sea creature that breathes air and has to come on land to have its babies.

Seat

The seat of a chair is the part that you sit on.

Seed

The seed of a plant or tree is in its flower, fruit or nut and it can grow into a young plant or tree.

See-saw

The two children can go up and down on the see-saw.

Settee

A settee is like a large chair for two or three people; it is also known as a sofa.

Shadow

If I shine a torch at the cat, you can see its shadow on the wall behind it.

Shape

Triangles, squares, circles and stars are all different shapes.

Shark

A shark is a fish that lives in the sea; there are many different kinds and some can grow very big.

Shears

Shears are like a very large pair of scissors that you use outside for cutting hedges and plants.

Sheep

Sheep are animals that are kept on the farm for their wool or for their meat.

Shelf

I keep books, my teddy bear, my alarm clock and all sorts of things on the **shelf** in my room.

Shell

Some small sea creatures have a **shell** to protect their bodies, and when the creature dies we may find the empty shell on the beach.

Shelter

We stand in the **shelter** while we wait for the bus to arrive.

Shield

A **shield** is used to protect your body from harm in battle.

Ship

A **ship** is a very large boat that nowadays is usually driven by powerful engines.

Shipwreck

In a severe storm, a ship can be beaten against rocks, resulting in a shipwreck.

Shoes

We wear shoes on our feet to protect them.

Shop

We can buy all sorts of delicious things in this shop!

Shower

I have a shower when I have been swimming; sometimes the water is very cold.

Showjumper

The showjumper must ride round the course without knocking down any fences to win the competition.

Signature

Our signature is the way we write our name when we sign a letter or a card.

Silver

Silver is a precious metal that can be used to make jewellery.

Skateboard

A skateboard is a platform on roller-skate wheels, that you ride and balance on.

abcdefghijklmnopqr**s**tuvwxyz

Skeleton

A skeleton is made up of the bones of an animal and is the frame for its muscles and flesh.

Sketch

I am doing a sketch, or a quick drawing, of this house.

Skis

Skis are the long thin strips of metal or plastic, attached to boots, which skiers wear to slide down a snowy slope.

Sky

The sky is the great expanse of air above our heads, where we can see the clouds, sun, moon and stars.

Sledge

If there has been enough snow we can have fun with our sledge.

Slide

We climb up the slide in our playground and we slip down again on our bottoms.

Smile

We smile when we are happy and want to show it.

Smoke

The leaves we are burning are still a little damp, so there is a lot of smoke which makes our eyes water.

Snail

A snail is a small creature that moves very slowly and carries its home, a shell, with it.

Snake

A snake is a reptile similar to a lizard but without any legs.

Snow

When there is a lot of snow on the ground we can build a snowman.

Soap

We use soap to wash our face and hands.

Socks

This pair of socks has been washed and is now drying on the line.

Soldier

A soldier wears a uniform, and is trained to fight in an army.

Somersault

After a lot of practising, I can do a somersault over the box in the gym.

Soot

The sweep is brushing out the chimney, and all the soot has landed on the hearth.

Spade

My dad uses the big spade when he is digging the flowerbeds.

Spaghetti

Long, thin spaghetti is made from a special flour and water dough, and it can be very difficult to eat!

Sparrow

Some sparrows have just flown on to the bird table to eat the bread.

Spider

A spider is an eight-legged creature that spins a web to catch its food.

Spoon

A spoon is a piece of cutlery that is used for eating soups and puddings and stirring drinks like tea and coffee.

Sports

Sports are the games that people play for fun or for work, such as football, tennis, golf, cricket and many others.

Square

A square is a shape with four sides of equal length, such as the shape of this window.

Squid

A squid is a sea creature without a skeleton, and it has ten arms round its mouth to catch its food.

abcdefghijklmnopqr**s**tuvwxyz

Squirrel

A **squirrel** has a long, bushy tail, and spends most of its life in the trees, eating nuts.

Stable

A **stable** is a special building where horses are kept.

Stadium

Some sports events are held at special places called **stadiums**, where thousands of people can sit and watch.

Stage

We watched the children perform their songs on the school **stage**.

Stain

When I opened the can the drink fizzed out and now I have a **stain** on my tee-shirt.

Staircase

A **staircase** in a building goes from one floor to another.

Stamp

I must put a **stamp** on my letter to make sure it will be delivered by the postman.

Starling

The **starling** is a wild bird that can copy other birds' songs. In the evening they fly in huge flocks to roost for the night.

Statue

The Statue of Liberty in New York harbour is a famous monument.

Steam

When a kettle of water boils, the white vapour that comes out of the spout is called steam.

Steeple

The steeple of a church is the tall tower with a pointed spire on top.

Stem

Flowers in the garden grow on stems, which we cut when we pick flowers to put in a vase.

Sticky tape

I'm trying to wrap a present for my friend, and now I've got sticky tape on everything except the paper.

Stone

Four thousand years ago, people built great circles like this with huge blocks of stone.

Stool

If I climb on this stool I can reach the chocolate cake that Mum made.

abcdefghijklmnopqrstuvwxyz

Stork

The white stork is a large wading bird that nests on chimneys and roofs; this is supposed to bring good luck.

Storm

A storm at sea can cause huge waves on the coast.

Story

When it's time for bed, Mum reads us a story.

Strawberry

The strawberry is a tasty fruit that can be eaten with cream, sugar or ice cream.

Stream

A stream flows past the bottom of our garden on its way to join a river.

Stretcher

Injured or ill people are carried on a stretcher.

Submarine

A submarine is built to travel underwater.

Sugar

We put sugar on our food or in a drink to make it taste sweeter.

Suit

We often wear a suit, either trousers and jacket for a man or skirt

and jacket for a lady, when we work in an office.

Suitcase

We put all our clothes in a suitcase when we travel.

Summit

When people climb a mountain, they are trying to reach the summit, or very top of it.

Sun

The setting sun makes the sky and clouds look red and orange.

Swamp

A swamp is a wet, warm and muddy place, with many unusual plants and trees.

abcdefghijklmnopqr**s**tuvwxyz

Swan

A **swan** is a beautiful water bird, whose young are called cygnets.

Sweet

Toffee and chocolate are **sweets**, and too many can be bad for your teeth!

Swimmer

I go swimming for fun, but these **swimmers** are trying to win the race.

Swing

We have a **swing** in our back garden that my little brother likes to play on.

Switch

There is a **switch** on the wall to turn the light on and off.

Sword

Swords were used by soldiers when they fought battles many years ago.

t is for transport

People use transport to get from place to place, on **land**, **sea** or in the **air**.

Air:

People are **flown** from an **airport** or **airfield** by a **pilot**.

Aeroplane

Helicopter

Sea:

People **sail** on **ships** with a **crew** of **sailors** from a **port** or **harbour**. People can also sail their **boats** on **rivers** and **lakes**.

Ship

Barge

Land:

People travel on **roads** or **railways**. They can **drive** themselves or be driven by someone else. Most people cannot drive a **railway train** but lots of people can drive a **car**.

Train

How many more transport words can you find in the dictionary?

Ambulance

Taxi

Tt

Table

I'm putting the cutlery on the table ready for our tea.

Tadpole

Tadpoles are baby frogs. As their legs grow, their tails disappear.

Tail

These lemurs have very bushy striped tails.

Tambourine

I can hit or shake my tambourine in time to music.

Tank

A tank is an armoured vehicle that runs on caterpillar tracks to get over rough ground.

Tankard

People used to drink beer from the antique tankards which my grandfather collects.

Tapestry

Tapestry is a kind of embroidery worked on a special material.

abcdefghijklmnopqrstuvwxyz

Target

I hit the bull's-eye on the target with one of my arrows.

Taxi

We travelled in a black taxi when we went to London.

Teacher

Today the teacher is talking to us about shapes and has drawn some on the blackboard.

Teeth

A lion has a set of very sharp pointed teeth!

Telephone

My big sister is always talking to her friends on the telephone, and Dad has just seen the latest bill!

Telescope

With my telescope, I can look at distant things like ships at sea or even the sky at night.

Tennis

Tennis is a game played on a tennis court by two or four people, with rackets and a ball.

abcdefghijklmnopqrstuvwxyz

Tent

We are camping in a field and the first thing to do is to put up our **tent**.

Thatch

A thatcher uses straw or reeds to make the **thatch** on the roof of an old building like this.

Theatre

We go to our town **theatre** to see plays and shows.

Thermometer

A **thermometer** tells us the temperature of something; that is how hot or cold it is.

Thimble

I wear a **thimble** on my finger to protect it when I am sewing.

Thorn

This rose bush has very sharp **thorns**.

Thread

I need a needle and **thread** to do my sewing.

Throne

A **throne** is a richly decorated chair that a king or queen uses on special occasions.

abcdefghijklmnopqrstuvwxyz

Thrush

The thrush feeds on snails and breaks their shells open on a stone.

Thunderstorm

We rushed to get out of the heavy rain when the thunderstorm started.

Ticket

I have just given in my ticket to show that my journey has been paid for.

Tie

My brother has his school tie on and Dad is wearing a spotted bow tie today.

Tiger

The tiger is the largest member of the cat family and has a beautiful striped coat.

Timber

When trees are cut down to be used for building or making things, the wood is called timber.

Toad

A toad is like a frog but it walks or crawls and has a warty skin.

Tongue

The dog's tongue flops out of its mouth because it is panting.

Torch

We have had a power cut so I use my torch to light the way upstairs.

Tortoise

A tortoise is a reptile whose body is inside a shell.

Towel

I am using a blue towel to dry my face.

Tower

A tower is a tall building like this famous leaning one in Pisa, Italy, or is part of another building like a castle.

Town

A town is a collection of buildings that is bigger than a village but smaller than a city.

Toy

I like to play with my **toys**; today I have chosen two dolls and my teddy.

Tractor

The seagulls are following the **tractor** as it pulls the plough across the field.

Traffic

Now that many people have cars, there is more **traffic** on the roads and motorways.

Train

A **train** runs on a track, taking passengers from city to city, across the country.

Trampoline

My young brother loves to bounce on the **trampoline** on his own.

Trapeze

The circus performers on the **trapeze** are swinging high above the audience.

abcdefghijklmnopqrstuvwxyz

Tray

If I'm not careful, the drinks and cakes will slide off the tray I'm carrying.

Treasure

The pirates opened the chest to find the treasure inside.

Tree

A tree is a large, tall plant with a trunk, which grows thousands of leaves and can produce nuts or fruit.

Triangle

This musical instrument is called a triangle because it has three sides which makes three angles.

Tricycle

My little brother has been given a tricycle, or three-wheeled bike, to ride.

Trowel

The builder uses a trowel to help him cement the bricks together.

Truck

This **truck** is being used to move large amounts of earth.

Trumpet

The **trumpet** is a brass musical instrument that you blow.

Trunk

I can keep things in a **trunk**, an elephant's long nose is called a **trunk**, and the widest part of a tree is also called its **trunk**.

Tube

I am squeezing white paint out of this **tube** to mix with the other colours on my palette.

Tug

A **tug** is a small boat that is used to tow large ships in and out of a harbour.

Tunnel

A subway is a **tunnel** which we walk through to go safely under the busy main road.

abcdefghijklmnopqrstuvwxyz

Turban

In some countries, men wear a turban on their head.

Turkey

A turkey is a large farm bird.

Turtle

A turtle is a reptile like a tortoise, but it spends its life in water.

Tusk

The walrus is one animal that has tusks or long teeth.

Twins

These two brothers look exactly the same as each other because they are identical twins.

Typewriter

I type all my letters on my typewriter.

Tyre

We had a flat tyre on the car and Dad had to change it before we could go out.

Uu

Umbrella

We shelter underneath an **umbrella** when it rains.

Unicorn

A **unicorn** in stories and legends is a horse-like creature with a spiral horn on its head.

Uniform

People working in many different jobs have to wear a **uniform**; nurses, police and firemen are three but there are plenty of others.

Universe

The **universe** is all of space and its contents, where the galaxy with our solar system is just one of many.

Vv

Valley

A river runs at the bottom of the **valley**.

Vase

A **vase** is a pretty pot or glass container for cut flowers.

Vehicle

Cars, buses, lorries and vans are all types of **vehicle**.

Veil

In some countries, women wear a **veil** over their faces when they go outside.

Violet

A **violet** is a small spring plant that has sweetly-scented flowers.

Violin

A **violin** is a musical instrument with strings which you play with a bow.

Volcano

Molten rock pours down the side of a **volcano** when it erupts.

w is for our world

Ww   Space

Space is all around the Earth above the air, which we call the atmosphere. The Earth is part of the group of planets round our Sun, which is called the solar system.

The Planets

Mercury	Venus	Earth	Mars	
Jupiter	Saturn	Uranus	Neptune	Pluto

The Sun

Our Sun is a star in a big group of stars called a galaxy. Our galaxy is called the Milky Way. Space is full of other planets, stars and galaxies.

The Earth

The Earth is made up of sea and land. There are five large areas of water called oceans. They are called the Atlantic, Pacific, Indian, Arctic and Antarctic Oceans.

There are seven large land masses called continents. They are called Africa, Asia, Europe, The Americas, Antarctica and Australia.

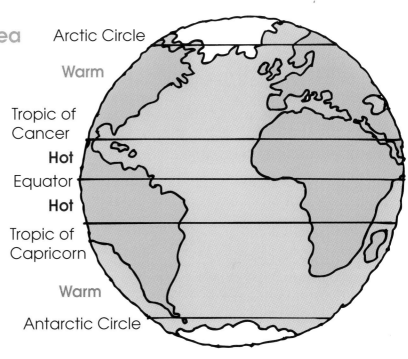

Cold
Arctic Circle
Warm
Tropic of Cancer
Hot
Equator
Hot
Tropic of Capricorn
Warm
Antarctic Circle
Cold

There are imaginary lines drawn round the world which show where the weather is hot, warm or cold.

Ww

Wagon

This old **wagon** needs a horse to pull it along.

Waiter

The **waiter** in the restaurant takes the orders and serves the food.

Wall

There is a very high brick **wall** round the village school.

Wallet

My father keeps his money in his leather **wallet**.

Wasp

Wasps are insects that love sweet foods, like jam, and they can give you a painful sting.

Watch

We wear a **watch** to tell us the time.

Waterfall

A **waterfall** is formed when there is a steep drop in the path of a river.

Weapon

These are all old-fashioned types of weapon that are no longer used.

Weasel

A weasel is a small wild animal which hunts for its food mainly at night.

Weed

This dandelion is a weed, a wild plant that grows where it is not wanted!

Well

A well is a deep hole in the ground that provides water, which is pulled up in a bucket.

Whale

The blue whale is the largest creature in the world today, and it lives in the sea, swimming great distances.

Wheat

Ripe wheat is harvested and the grains are ground to make flour.

Wheel

This wheel has to be mended before it can be put back on the tractor.

abcdefghijklmnopqrstuvwxyz

Wheelbarrow

The gardener uses his **wheelbarrow** to carry garden rubbish, and the dog wants a ride!

Whistle

When I blow this **whistle** the game will be finished.

Wig

A **wig** is false hair worn over our own hair. Some lawyers, called barristers, wear white wigs when they are in court.

Wigwam

A **wigwam** is another word for a tepee, the traditional home of the North American Indians.

Windmill

A **windmill** uses the wind to turn its sails for grinding corn.

Window

The cat is waiting for someone to open the **window** to let him in.

abcdefghijklmnopqrstuvwxyz

Wing

Birds have special feathers on their **wings** which help them fly through the air.

Witch

A **witch**, in stories, flies on a broomstick and has a black cat as her companion.

Wizard

According to stories a **wizard** can make magic potions and cast spells.

Wolf

A **wolf** is a member of the dog family which has yellow eyes and a thick coat.

Wood

A **wood** is an area where trees and plants grow thickly, with many birds and small animals living in it.

Woodpecker

The **woodpecker** pecks a hole in a tree to make its nest, and feeds on grubs and insects in the bark.

abcdefghijklmnopqrstuvwxyz

Wool

Wool is a thread spun from a sheep's fleece that we use for knitting and weaving.

World

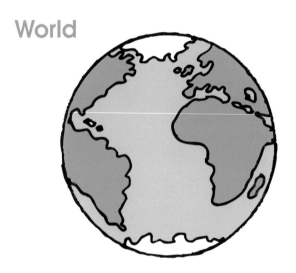

Our planet Earth, the third planet from the Sun is also called the World.

Worm

We need worms in the garden to help break up the soil.

Wreath

We made a Christmas wreath, or garland, to go on our front door.

Wren

The tiny wren has a short, turned-up tail and a loud song.

X-ray

An **x-ray** is a special picture that lets us see inside our bodies.

Xylophone

A **xylophone** is a musical instrument with wooden bars of different lengths which are hit with small hammers.

X also comes at the end of some words like o**x**, bo**x**, fo**x** and fi**x**.

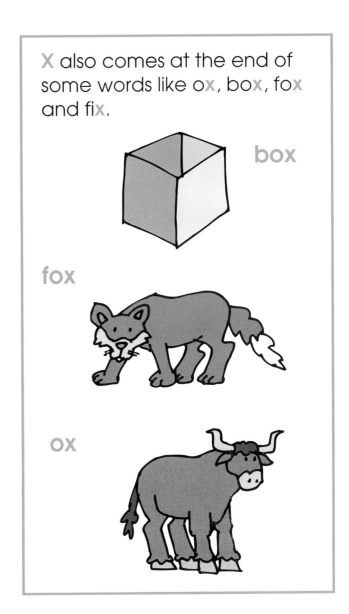

box

fox

ox

Yy

Yacht

These **yachts** speed across the water when the wind blows in their sails.

Yak

A **yak** is a type of ox with a thick coat that is still used to carry loads in some countries.

Yawn

When I'm tired, I give a great big **yawn**.

Yoghurt

Yoghurt is a food made of milk and it often has fruit in it.

Yoke

The milkmaid carries her milk-churns on a **yoke** across her shoulders.
A **yoke** is also used to join two oxen to help them pull a cart.

Yolk

The **yolk** of an egg is the yellow part in the middle.

Yo-yo

A **yo-yo** is a round toy which can be made to run up and down a string attached to it.

Young

The babies of an animal are called its **young**. This pig's young are the piglets.

Zz

Zebra

A **zebra** is a wild animal which looks like a horse with black and white stripes.

Zero

Jack has missed the board with his three darts and his score is **zero**, or nothing!

Zigzag

A **zigzag** is a line that goes sharply from side to side.

Zip

A **zip** has two strips of plastic or metal teeth that lock together and it is used to fasten our clothes.

Zoo

We go to the **zoo** to see many different kinds of wild animals.

Parts of the body

There are special words for parts of your body.

hair
forehead
eye
eyebrow
cheek
nose
mouth
teeth
chin

head
ear
neck
shoulder
arm
fist
face
knee
leg
ankle

chest
tummy
wrist

thumb
finger
hand
elbow
back

calf

heel
toe
thigh
foot
bottom

The Family

There are special names for people in the family. These names let people know how everyone is related to each other. You can show this by a special diagram called a family tree.

My name is Matthew Jones. This is a photograph of me and my dog.

My parents are Mr and Mrs Jones. I call them Mummy and Daddy. They have three children including me.

My Mummy and Daddy's parents are my grandparents. We are their grandchildren.

Grandpa Smith
Grandma Smith

Mr *and* Mrs Jones

Grandad Jones
Granny Jones

Auntie Annie

Anthony Jones

Katie Jones

Uncle Bill, Auntie Sally, Robin *and* Rachel

My Mummy has a twin sister. Her name is Annie Smith. She is our auntie. My brother and I are her nephews. My sister is her niece.

This is me with my brother and my sister.

My Daddy has a brother called Bill. He is married to Sally. They are our uncle and aunt. They have two children who are our cousins. Robin is my parents' nephew, Rachel is my parents' niece.

121

Colours and Numbers

Colours

An artist mixes the colours in his tubes of paint to paint a picture.

Red, **yellow** and **blue** are called the **primary** colours.

Orange, **green** and **purple** are called the **secondary** colours. These are mixed from the primary colours.

Red

Orange

Purple

Blue   Yellow

Green

If he adds **black** or **white** he can make other **darker** or **lighter** colours.

Numbers

1   **One red** rose

2   **Two blue** birds

3   **Three purple** planets

4   **Four white** rabbits

5   **Five pink** flamingos

6   **Six green** dinosaurs

7   **Seven orange** teddy bears

8   **Eight yellow** chicks

9   **Nine black** cats

10   **Ten scarlet** soldiers

122

20 Two sets of ten soldiers will make twenty.

30 Three sets of ten soldiers will make thirty.

40 Four sets of ten soldiers will make forty.

50 Five sets of ten soldiers will make fifty.

60 Six sets of ten soldiers will make sixty.

70 Seven sets of ten soldiers will make seventy.

80 Eight sets of ten soldiers will make eighty.

90 Nine sets of ten soldiers will make ninety.

10 Ten sets of ten soldiers will make one hundred.

100 One hundred

This Roman soldier was called a centurion because he was in charge of 100 soldiers. Our word century, which means 100 years, comes from the Latin word for one hundred.

1000 One thousand

If there were 10 times as many Roman soldiers there would be an army of 1000 soldiers with a general to command them.

123

The Year

Months

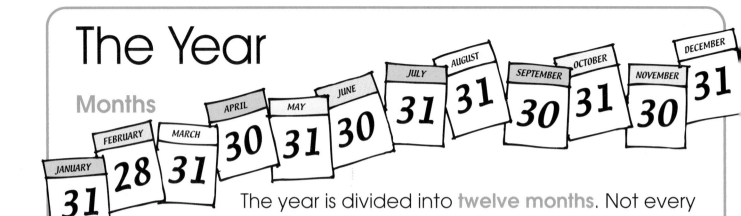

The year is divided into twelve months. Not every month has the same number of days but all the days add up to three hundred and sixty five.

Weeks

A month is divided into sets of seven days called weeks. You can write in a diary to remind you what you have to do on each day.

Days

There are twenty-four hours in a day. Most clocks show only twelve hours and the hands go round twice in a day. Some modern clocks show twenty-four hours.

Hours

Each hour is divided into sixty minutes. You need to set the timer on your video in hours and minutes if you want to record your favourite programme while you are out.

The Seasons

The year can also be divided into four seasons.

Spring   Summer   Autumn   Winter

Every year people have special days which are important to them. They do something special or celebrate some event that has happened in the past. We mark them on a **calendar** so that we will remember them.

Birthday

Holiday

School Sports Day

Christmas

Easter

Bonfire Night

Children who come from other lands have special days to celebrate religious festivals or to honour their homeland.

The Chinese New Year

People celebrate with fireworks and lion dances.

4th July

The special day when Americans celebrate **Independence Day**.

Chanukah (or Hanukkah)

An eight day Jewish religious festival. Each day a new candle is lit; the eight candles are lit from a ninth.

Ramadan

Thirty days when Muslims say special prayers and do not eat while it is daylight.

Diwali

A religious festival when Hindus light many candles.